My name is
Butterfly

Written by Mary Ellen Ryall
Illustrated by Stevie Marie Aubuchon-Mendoza

Especially for:

Story Copyright © 2011 Mary Ellen Ryall.
Illustrations Copyright © 2011 by Stevie Marie Aubuchon-Mendoza.
All Rights Reserved.
No part of this publication may be reproduced, stored in a retrieval system, or transmitted in any form or By any means without permission in writing from the publisher.

ISBN: 978-0-9816949-9-3

Printed in the USA
Salt of the Earth Press
Springbrook, Wisconsin, USA
www.saltpress.com

One warm, sunny morning in June, my mother landed on a native common milkweed plant in Sarah Reynolds' flower and vegetable garden. Sarah was a child with brown eyes and honey blonde straight hair.

She was in the garden one morning pulling weeds when she saw my mother. Sarah stood very still. She blinked in wonder as she watched my mother deposit eggs on the underside of the leaves.

After my mother flew off, Sarah sat down on the ground. She thought about what she had just seen. Excited, she turned her baseball cap around backwards and ran to the house to tell her mother.

"I saw a black and orange butterfly tap milkweed leaves with its tummy!" Sarah said.

Her mother said, "You saw a female Monarch butterfly laying her eggs. The butterfly wants to be sure each egg has plenty of milkweed leaves to eat when it hatches, so she only lays one egg under each leaf. In four to ten days they should hatch."

A few days later, Sarah went back to visit her garden. She touched some Black-eyed Susans, which were pretty yellow flowers with dark centers. Then she turned to the milkweed flowers and bent down to smell the sweet scent when she saw something.

Sarah looked right at me. I was now a tiny caterpillar munching a milkweed leaf. I was no bigger than a thumbnail.

Sarah said, "You sure are cute with your rings of yellow, black, and off-white." She saw the hole I had eaten through a milkweed leaf. She figured out that when my egg hatched I ate through the leaf and climbed to the top.

With an explorer's eye she looked more closely. Sarah saw several caterpillars munching away on different leaves. She looked at other milkweed plants and saw that the whole garden was a nursery for tiny Monarch caterpillars.

Sarah noticed her mother hanging clothes on the clothesline. The white sheets swayed in the wind on the balmy summer day. Sarah told her mother about the caterpillar nursery. Her mother told her letting milkweed grow in the garden helped Monarch butterflies. Monarch caterpillars only ate milkweed leaves. The flower and vegetable garden was a good place for the butterflies, because it was organic and healthy. Her mother told Sarah that herbicides and pesticides could harm butterflies and other helpful pollinating insects like bees.

My life continued and every day I continued to grow. I shed my skin several times, which is normal for a baby butterfly. This is called molting. One late afternoon after a gentle rainstorm, Sarah came out to the garden to check on me. She looked and looked and couldn't find me, even though I had grown quite big.

"Where are you?" Sarah called. She got down on her hands and knees on the wet straw and looked on the underside of milkweed leaves. There I was sleeping peacefully, all safe and snug. With a joyful heart Sarah said, "So there you are!"

The next day, Sarah's mother came out to the garden. She smiled at Sarah as her daughter watched a Monarch caterpillar.

Sarah's mother told her, "Did you know that another name for caterpillar is larva? Your butterfly larva will grow and change until it hangs upside down from a leaf like a tiny J." Meanwhile, I knew that after two or three weeks as a caterpillar, I was going to have to find another place to change into the next stage of my life.

I found a plant nearby so that Sarah could find me. I crawled to a bean plant on my little pads and there I spun a silken thread on the underside of a leaf. I hung from the leaf with my body curved so I was in the shape of a J. My skin split and I wriggled out of it. This time it was different from the other times I molted! Beneath the skin was a hard protective shell. It would keep me safe now that I was no longer a butterfly. I had become a pupa. Sarah and her mother left the garden and went into the house for lunch.

The next day, Sarah came to the garden. To her dismay, she couldn't find me. She ran to the house to tell her mother. Her mother said, "Caterpillars just want to go off to someplace quiet when they turn into a pupa."

Sarah asked, "Why do they go away?"

Her mother told her, "Birds and other creatures that might want to eat Monarch caterpillars know to look for milkweed. So when it's time for the caterpillar to change, it goes far away from its home. That way they are safer."

Each day Sarah kept visiting the garden. Even the happy flower faces didn't cheer her up. She said, "I'll pull weeds around the bean plants and make the garden beautiful." All of a sudden, a hummingbird approached and started sipping nectar from a Tiger lily. The sight of the hummingbird made Sarah feel better.

Then Sarah looked at the bean plant where I was hiding. She was thrilled when she realized it was me. I had changed into a lime-colored jewel dangling from the underside of the bean leaf. She was amazed when she saw three golden dots and the golden band around the upper part of my pupa. Her mother had told her that a butterfly pupa has a hard skin. A butterfly pupa with that protective shell is also called a chrysalis. That was the green jewel she saw!

Sarah visited me daily watching the drama of my unfolding birth. I remained in the pupa for nearly two weeks. Sarah watched as my chrysalis changed from light green to a dark color. My wings were developing color within the pupa and this is what Sarah was seeing. Sarah realized that soon I would be born as she saw me turn darker and darker. My chrysalis turned paper-thin when I was ready to be born. I waited until the sun warmed the chrysalis and it was dry. It is then that I burst through the shell and emerged as a full-grown Monarch butterfly.

The corn stalks were rustling in the wind. I was born a few minutes before Sarah arrived in the garden. She was so happy to see me! I was only a few minutes old. I was exhausted and my wings were wet. I had to fight the wind and cling to the bean plant. If I fell to the ground I would be vulnerable to birds. My feet grasped the stalk as I slowly grew in strength. I began to pump fluid from my tummy into my wings to dry them.

Sarah whispered to me, "I love you. You are so beautiful."

Then I dried the underside of my wings by wrapping them around my body like I was hugging myself. I could feel Sarah near me and knew I wanted to share these first hours of my life with her. You see, I was her teacher.

Sarah noticed the two black spots on my wings and realized I was a male butterfly. In about three hours I had climbed from the bean plant and neared the top of a sunflower. There I rested while the sun warmed and further dried my wings. I weighed no more than a maple leaf!

Sarah watched as I clung to life in the high wind. She said, "You're very strong."

I didn't want to leave Sarah, but butterflies have to be free. I was born late in August and I would have to leave soon on a very long journey, but I could wait one day to visit with Sarah. She had a beautiful garden. Her mother had told her that butterflies sip the nectar inside flowers. Nectar is a sweet drink flowers hide inside themselves so that butterflies and bees will come to them.

The garden had native wild bergamot, common milkweed, coneflower, sunflower, Black-eyed Susan, and perennial Tiger Lily and sedum for me to choose from even though I didn't need nectar so soon after being born. I would need flower nectar in about a day.

Sarah enjoyed seeing me flitting about the flowers, but she knew that we had to say goodbye soon. The sun was setting in the west behind the old Jack Pine tree and I wanted to be high and roost in a tree for the night.

Sarah said, "I want to give you a name before you fly away." I landed on a sunflower, turned my head to her, and she whispered, "Your name is Mariposa. That means butterfly in Spanish."

After my naming ceremony, it was time for me to fly to Mexico where I would spend the winter hibernating in the Oyamel Fir forest, deep within the mountains. I was leaving my memory behind with my friend. Sarah waved and promised, "I will always remember you."

Mary Ellen Ryall grew up in Saratoga Springs, New York. In pursuit of butterflies, she worked and traveled in South America in the 1970s. In the 1980s Ryall completed the Master Gardeners Program, University of the District of Columbia, and became involved with community gardens. Living in Southern Maryland in the 1990s, she wrote about the environment and founded Happy Tonics. Ryall moved to Wisconsin in 2000, graduating from the Woodlands Wisdom Nutrition Project at Lac Courte Oreilles Ojibwa Community College in 2003. In 2006 Ryall relocated the organization to Shell Lake, Wisconsin where she spearheaded the implementation of a Monarch Butterfly Habitat.

Stevie Marie Aubuchon-Mendoza lives with her family outside the glitz and glamour of Las Vegas, Nevada. She is inspired by the dusty, desert landscape and the secrets that it holds. When she isn't painting dinosaurs and dragons, she loves having tea parties and playing in the dirt with her young daughter.

Happy Tonics, Inc. is a nonprofit 501 (c)(3) Environmental Education Organization and Public Charity. A Monarch Butterfly Habitat was created on city land in Shell Lake, Wisconsin in 2008. The project was made possible with assistance of the U.S. Fish and Wildlife Service and a donation of native wildflower and grass seed from Crex Meadow and Cheboygan National Forest. The habitat is alongside Highway 63 on the lakeside and a few blocks north of downtown Shell Lake.

www.happytonics.org

Made in the USA
Charleston, SC
13 August 2011